D1335987

FRANCIS FRITH'S

THE WIRRAL

PHOTOGRAPHIC MEMORIES

JIM RUBERY has lived in Yorkshire since 1975, having moved to the south of the county after being educated in the Midlands. He is a very keen participant in outdoor pursuits, and has spent a great deal of his spare time over the years climbing, mountaineering, walking, skiing, and canoeing, and has even dabbled with caving and sailing. He started writing for the climbing press in the early 1990s, and he has had a regular walking column, entitled 'Rambling with Rubery', in *Cheshire Life* magazine since 1997. This is also now a regular monthly feature in the sister magazines *Yorkshire Life* and *Lancashire Life*. Wherever possible, Jim tries to incorporate a place of interest along the way in his walks, often a historic building or area of archaeological importance. It is from this that his love of historical places has grown, whether it is a prehistoric stone circle, a ruined castle or abbey from medieval times or a relatively modern building from the Industrial Revolution.

FRANCIS FRITH'S
PHOTOGRAPHIC MEMORIES

THE WIRRAL

PHOTOGRAPHIC MEMORIES

JIM RUBERY

First published in the United Kingdom in 2003 by
Frith Book Company Ltd

Paperback Edition 2003
ISBN 1-85937-517-0

British Library Cataloguing in Publication Data

Photographic Memories - The Wirral
Jim Rubery

Frith Book Company Ltd
Frith's Barn, Teffont,
Salisbury, Wiltshire SP3 5QP
Tel: +44 (0) 1722 716 376
Email: info@francisfrith.co.uk
www.francisfrith.co.uk

Printed and bound in Great Britain

Front Cover: **WALLASEY,** *May Cottage and the Nook 1898*
W164012
Frontispiece: **EGREMONT,** *Promenade 1912* 64439

*The colour-tinting is for illustrative purposes only, and is not intended to be
historically accurate*

AS WITH ANY HISTORICAL DATABASE THE FRITH ARCHIVE IS CONSTANTLY
BEING CORRECTED AND IMPROVED AND THE PUBLISHERS WOULD
WELCOME INFORMATION ON OMISSIONS OR INACCURACIES

CONTENTS

FRANCIS FRITH
VICTORIAN PIONEER

FRANCIS FRITH, founder of the world-famous photographic archive, was a complex and multi-talented man. A devout Quaker and a highly successful Victorian businessman, he was philosophic by nature and pioneering in outlook.

By 1855 he had already established a wholesale grocery business in Liverpool, and sold it for the astonishing sum of £200,000, which is the equivalent today of over £15,000,000. Now a very rich man, he was able to indulge his passion for travel. As a child he had pored over travel books written by early explorers, and his fancy and imagination had been stirred by family holidays to the sublime mountain regions of Wales and Scotland. 'What lands of spirit-stirring and enriching scenes and places!' he had written. He was to return to these scenes of grandeur in later years to 'recapture the thousands of vivid and tender memories', but with a different purpose. Now in his thirties, and captivated by the new science of photography, Frith set out on a series of pioneering journeys up the Nile and to the Near East that occupied him from 1856 until 1860.

INTRIGUE AND EXPLORATION

These far-flung journeys were packed with intrigue and adventure. In his life story, written when he was sixty-three, Frith tells of being held captive by bandits, and of fighting 'an awful midnight battle to the very point of surrender with a deadly pack of hungry, wild dogs'. Wearing flowing Arab costume, Frith arrived at Akaba by camel seventy years before Lawrence of Arabia, where he encountered 'desert princes and rival sheikhs, blazing with jewel-hilted swords'.

He was the first photographer to venture beyond the sixth cataract of the Nile. Africa was still the mysterious 'Dark Continent', and Stanley and Livingstone's historic meeting was a decade into the future. The conditions for picture taking confound belief. He laboured for hours in his wicker dark-room in the sweltering heat of the desert, while the volatile chemicals fizzed dangerously in their trays. Back in London he exhibited his photographs and was 'rapturously cheered' by members of the Royal Society. His reputation as a photographer was made overnight.

VENTURE OF A LIFE-TIME

Characteristically, Frith quickly spotted the opportunity to create a new business as a specialist publisher of photographs. He lived in an era of immense and sometimes violent change.

For the poor in the early part of Victoria's reign work was exhausting and the hours long, and people had precious little free time to enjoy themselves. Most had no transport other than a cart or gig at their disposal, and rarely travelled far beyond the boundaries of their own town or village. However, by the 1870s the railways had threaded their way across the country, and Bank Holidays and half-day Saturdays had been made obligatory by Act of Parliament. All of a sudden the working man and his family were able to enjoy days out and see a little more of the world.

With typical business acumen, Francis Frith foresaw that these new tourists would enjoy having souvenirs to commemorate their days out. In 1860 he married Mary Ann Rosling and set out on a new career: his aim was to photograph every city, town and village in Britain. For the next thirty years he travelled the country by train and by pony and trap, producing fine photographs of seaside resorts and beauty spots that were keenly bought by millions of Victorians. These prints were painstakingly pasted into family albums and pored over during the dark nights of winter, rekindling precious memories of summer excursions.

THE RISE OF FRITH & CO

Frith's studio was soon supplying retail shops all over the country. To meet the demand he gathered about him a small team of photographers, and published the work of independent artist-photographers of the calibre of Roger Fenton and Francis Bedford. In order to gain some understanding of the scale of Frith's business one only has to look at the catalogue issued by Frith & Co in 1886: it runs to some 670 pages, listing not only many thousands of views of the British Isles but also many photographs of most European countries, and China, Japan, the USA and Canada - note the sample page shown on page 9 from the hand-written Frith & Co ledgers recording the pictures. By 1890 Frith had created the greatest specialist photographic publishing company in the world, with over 2,000 sales outlets - more than the combined number that Boots and WH Smith have today! The picture on the next page shows the Frith & Co display board at Ingleton in the Yorkshire Dales (left of window). Beautifully constructed with a mahogany frame and gilt inserts, it could display up to a dozen local scenes.

POSTCARD BONANZA

The ever-popular holiday postcard we know today took many years to develop. In 1870 the Post Office issued the first plain cards, with a pre-printed stamp on one face. In 1894 they allowed other publishers' cards to be sent through the mail with an attached adhesive halfpenny stamp. Demand grew rapidly, and in 1895 a new size of postcard was permitted called the court card, but there was little room for illustration. In 1899, a year after Frith's death, a new card measuring 5.5 x 3.5 inches became the standard format, but it was not until 1902 that the divided back came into being, so that the address and message could be on one face and a full-size illustration on the other. Frith & Co were in the vanguard of postcard development: Frith's sons Eustace and Cyril continued their father's monumental task, expanding the number of views offered to the public and recording more and more places in

Britain, as the coasts and countryside were opened up to mass travel.

Francis Frith had died in 1898 at his villa in Cannes, his great project still growing. The archive he created continued in business for another seventy years. By 1970 it contained over a third of a million pictures showing 7,000 British towns and villages.

FRANCIS FRITH'S LEGACY

Frith's legacy to us today is of immense significance and value, for the magnificent archive of evocative photographs he created provides a unique record of change in the cities, towns and villages throughout Britain over a century and more. Frith and his fellow studio photographers revisited locations many times down the years to update their views, compiling for us an enthralling and colourful pageant of British life and character.

We are fortunate that Frith was dedicated to recording the minutiae of everyday life. For it is this sheer wealth of visual data, the painstaking chronicle of changes in dress, transport, street layouts, buildings, housing, engineering and landscape that captivates us so much today. His remarkable images offer us a powerful link with the past and with the lives of our ancestors.

THE VALUE OF THE ARCHIVE TODAY

Computers have now made it possible for Frith's many thousands of images to be accessed almost instantly. Frith's images are increasingly used as visual resources, by social historians, by researchers into genealogy and ancestry, by architects and town planners, and by teachers involved in local history projects.

In addition, the archive offers every one of us an opportunity to examine the places where we and our families have lived and worked down the years. Highly successful in Frith's own era, the archive is now, a century and more on, entering a new phase of popularity. Historians consider the Francis Frith Collection to be of prime national importance. It is the only archive of its kind remaining in private ownership. Francis Frith's archive is now housed in an historic timber barn in the beautiful village of Teffont in Wiltshire. Its founder would not recognize the archive office as it is today. In place of the many thousands of dusty boxes containing glass plate negatives and an all-pervading odour of photographic chemicals, there are now ranks of computer screens. He would be amazed to watch his images travelling round the world at unimaginable speeds through internet lines.

The archive's future is both bright and exciting. Francis Frith, with his unshakeable belief in making photographs available to the greatest number of people, would undoubtedly approve of what is being done today with his lifetime's work. His photographs depicting our shared past are now bringing pleasure and enlightenment to millions around the world a century and more after his death.

THE WIRRAL
AN INTRODUCTION

Though now quite industrialised, particularly along its Mersey shoreline, the Wirral was not well endowed with raw materials and sources of power, unlike many other industrial regions in Britain. As a consequence of this, it was not one of the fore-runners of the Industrial Revolution. The reason for the explosion in the Wirral's population and the massive expansion of towns like Birkenhead, Ellesmere Port, Wallasey and Eastham was due to their proximity to the River Mersey.

Liverpool, literally just a short ferry ride across the Mersey from Wirral, developed into Britain's second greatest port during the 19th and 20th centuries. With its proximity to the industrial towns of the North and Midlands, the navigability of the River Mersey, and the easy access which that gave to the Atlantic Ocean and hence the British Empire and the rest of the world, it is easy to see why.

The towns along Wirral's eastern shoreline

GREAT MEOLS, *Station Approach c1955* M191027

expanded in parallel with their great Merseyside neighbour; this was not as a result of their muscling in on Liverpool's trade, but as a direct consequence of other factors that contributed to its infrastructure. Labour was available, a good transport network existed, land for industrial and domestic development close to the Mersey was in abundance, and there was a massive opportunity to house and process raw materials and finished products from elsewhere. Wirral was on to a winner. Between 1800 and the early 1900s, the population of Birkenhead rose from almost 700 to nearly 200,000, of Ellesmere Port from a little under 300 to over 10,000, and of Wallasey from just over 600 to 78,000.

Until 1974, the Wirral was situated in Cheshire, but the boundary reforms of that year meant that much of the Wirral went to the newly created Merseyside; the new county boundary ran from just north of Ellesmere Port in the east, across to Heswall in the west. Needless to say, many residents resented leaving Cheshire, despite the fact that many places were closer both geographically and economically to the South Lancashire towns, including Liverpool, that made up the rest of the new borough. However, the aggrieved residents were somewhat placated in 1986 when Margaret Thatcher's Conservative government abolished Merseyside; for administrative purposes, the area later became known as 'Wirral' once more.

Pre-Historic Wirral

Though now laced with an excellent road network and good rail and water links, and being in close proximity to both Liverpool and Manchester airports, the Wirral has not always

been so accessible. For centuries it was a wild, unwelcoming place, covered in forests in the main, but also with extensive bogs and marshes on its river margins. The first evidence of human life on the Wirral is found around 11,000 years ago in the Mesolithic or Middle Stone Age period. These people would have been hunter-gatherers, small nomadic groups living in temporary encampments and scouring the region's woods, beaches and marshes for deer, wild boar, berries, fruits and of course fish, particularly shellfish. The evidence for the existence of these people comes from numerous microliths (flakes knapped from flints when making tools), which have been found in many places, and the occasional tool find.

It was some 5,000 years later, in the Neolithic or New Stone Age and on into the Bronze and Iron Ages, that settlements became more permanent. Archaeologists have unearthed such sites at Meols, Greasby, Irby and Burton. These early residents would have started to shape the Wirral's physiognomy by clearing woodland to create fields and to provide fuel and building materials, and by moving rocks and stones to make huts and boundaries - and, of course, to create their ritual landscape of burial mounds and standing stones.

Geology and Geography

One of the most notable points about the Wirral, and one which has helped to shape its land forms, are the area's rich, red sandstones. These compressed sediments have been labelled by geologists as 'New Red Sandstones', an odd term considering that they were deposited hundreds of millions of years ago, but one which distinguishes them from older deposits of previous epochs. These sandstones, the uppermost of which were laid down about 200 million years ago, not only form the Wirral's hills – at Bidston, Caldy, Grange, Heswall, Storeton, Thurstaston and Wallasey – but have been used over the centuries to construct many of the region's most important and beautiful buildings, some of which appear in this photographic history.

The Romano-British people of the Wirral certainly knew that the local sandstone made excellent building material; the crystals of sparkling silica that course through its fine sand-grains probably added to their liking of it. The sandstones vary greatly in colour from area to area and from age to age, a feature that has been noted by many architects, who have combined this colour sequence into the stonework of a number of buildings. Many fossilised footprints from long extinct creatures have been found in the various strata, some of which were incorporated into buildings as an added attraction, for instance in the porch at Bebington church.

Besides the importance of the underlying rocks in shaping the Wirral's landscape, water too has had a massive impact. The Wirral is an excellent example of a peninsula (from the Latin 'paene insula', meaning 'almost an island'), with water on three sides. To the west is the lovely River Dee, with its expansive estuary that is so important to wildlife in the area; to the east is the mighty River Mersey, with its docks and factories; and to the north is that part of the Irish Sea known as Liverpool Bay. All have played a massive part in the region's past and present, and no doubt will play a part in its future. The Romans expanded the harbour at Meols on the north coast, while before the silting up of the Dee estuary, Neston,

Parkgate and West Kirby have all been important ports in their time; the Mersey shore has already been mentioned.

Roman Wirral

With the coming of the Romans in AD43, Britain was brought out of prehistory into history, but very little written evidence exists about the Wirral at this time. It would appear that the Roman occupation of the Wirral was not so much of a conquest, as more a gentle absorbing of the region into the Roman Empire. There were no great battles and no uprisings of note, and people went about their everyday business much as before.

Because of the remoteness of the Wirral and the general lassitude of life on the peninsula, it is highly likely that some locals saw the opportunity to improve their lot with a little entrepreneurial manoeuvring. By moving to the expanding Deva (Chester), numerous business opportunities would have presented themselves around the bustling Roman fortress.

Despite the fact that the Romans were in the region until the end of the 4th century, very little trace of their passing has been found. Pottery and coins from the period have been unearthed, and there may have been a Roman road linking Chester with Birkenhead and the port of Meols on the north coast, but little else has come to light.

The Dark Ages

Without the control and stability that had been imposed by the Roman army, the British people carried out their lives as best they could, Wirral being no different to the rest of the country.

Because of its still relatively isolated position, the area did not suffer the great upheavals that were affecting southern and eastern England with invasions of Angles, Saxons, Jutes and Danes.

Evidence would suggest that the Wirral was inhabited by Celts for about 200 years after the Romans left. They mainly spoke a Celtic language (an ancestor of modern Welsh), lived in distinct settlements, and practised the Christian religion. After this time, the Anglo-Saxons slowly moved into the area, infiltrating the local tongue with their Germanic language, renaming many of the villages, and creating the regional boundaries which remained more or less unchanged until 1974. A period of Scandinavian colonisation then followed. Some settlements were taken over, others were renamed, and new ones were established, and much marginal land was brought into cultivation.

The Great Medieval Hunting Forests

In October 1066, William Duke of Normandy defeated the English King Harold, the sequel of which was twenty years of violence, destruction, oppression and theft. In 1069, Yorkshire and Durham were ravaged, villages were burnt to the ground and many people massacred. Later in the same year the Normans crossed the Pennines into Cheshire and did much the same. Chester was wrecked, and the Wirral's manors wasted.

William gave the great estates to his many followers, leaving their previous owners and workers little option but to offer themselves as serfs to the Norman barons. Because the Wirral had large populations of deer and other game at the time, the area became a favoured hunting ground for the Norman kings and noblemen. A common sound at the time would have been that of the Wirral Horn, a brass-tipped hunting horn used by the foresters of the peninsula. It is today portrayed in many coats of arms associated with the Wirral originating from this time. For the next 200 years, feudalism and monasticism were to have extremely pervasive effects on both the landscape and human life.

The Tudors to the Victorians

When Henry Tudor defeated Richard III in 1485, he became regarded as England's first modern monarch. However, it was his second son, Henry VIII, who transformed English society. He dissolved the powerful monasteries, confiscated monastic lands and sold them, along with their properties, to secular landlords. He changed the country's religion and reformed its government; feudalism disappeared, a hierarchical structure for society evolved, and England became a nation state.

Over the next 300 years, monarchs were overthrown or succeeded, governments came and went, and a Civil War intervened in the affairs of all men, but no matter what your political persuasion or class of society to which you belonged, every person still had one thing in common – dependency on the land.

By the 1800s, almost all of the Wirral's woodland had been cleared for farming, and much marginal land on the Dee and Mersey estuaries had been drained for grazing. After farming, the second most important occupation in the Wirral was seafaring; this was largely confined to the Dee estuary, with Neston, Parkgate, and West Kirby all having ports or harbours. Unlike other regions in England, the Wirral had not yet been affected by the development of industry and the subsequent growth of its towns. But all was about to change.

Port Sunlight

Port Sunlight with its surrounding area holds great significance for local history and industrial archaeology. It is a 19th-century garden village built by William Hesketh Lever for the workers in his soap factory. Lever was a very benevolent employer who realised that contented workers meant improved productivity and better working relationships. To put Lever's vision into practice required the expertise of thirty different architects, who designed a unique environment in which people could live and work. The amenities include a school, a church, a hospital, a hotel, a technical institute, and an art gallery, and numerous open spaces, lawned areas and extensive flower beds.

Today, all the original buildings in the village are listed, and it is the only village of its type to retain its original boundaries. To complete its unique character, the village turns into a blaze of colour during the summer months when tubs, beds, borders and baskets are filled with the most wonderful flowers. The actual factory lies within the bounds of the village, behind a superb stone façade that completely disguises the extensive works that lies behind. The name of the village comes from the brand of fragrant soap that the factory was built to manufacture – 'Sunlight'.

The ideas that Lever had on sharing his prosperity are reflected in the fact that the Lever Brothers company subsidised not only the building of the village and its amenities, but their upkeep too. Another village in which Lever had a great input, and which reflects the architectural ideas seen in Port Sunlight, is Thornton Hough, just a few miles away in mid-Wirral.

The Wirral Today

Today, the peninsula is a place of many contrasts; just like the rest of Britain, the Wirral

EASTHAM, *Docks 1894* 33716

carries the evidence of its transmogrification from a rural to an industrial area, and thence to a post-industrial land. The River Mersey shoreline is still heavily industrialised, with Stanlow Oil Refinery, Vauxhall Motors, Bowaters Paper Mills, various docks and many other industries. Victorian working-class terraces and middle-class suburbs can still be seen in Birkenhead, Wallasey and Ellesmere Port, along with some very elegant coastal and country residences built by the well-heeled business entrepreneurs.

The coastal resorts are still there, but they are significantly changed from the way they were in the late 1800s up to the mid 1900s. However, there is a move to restore some of the attractions that

New Brighton once held. The interior of the Wirral has many areas that have changed little in recent times; there are extensive areas of farmland and heathland, quiet villages, cosy inns and sandy hills that afford wonderful views over the peninsula. The River Dee shoreline, where one can cast a glance across its broad acres to the misty hills of Wales on the far side, is a very tranquil place, with little or no industry to taint its natural beauty; here picturesque villages like Burton, Parkgate, Thurstaston and Caldy nestle. Unfortunately, the sea no longer laps at the footings of these villages, for the estuary silted up long ago; but like the rest of the world, the Wirral has changed, is changing and will continue to do so.

ELLESMERE PORT, *Whitby Road c1965* E135077

THE DEE ESTUARY

NESTON, *High Street 1939* N88006

We are looking south-east along Neston's main shopping street, with the wall of St Mary and St Helen's church on the immediate right. The road is still rather narrow and congested, but the scene has changed quite considerably in the intervening years, with many of the buildings being demolished, replaced or altered. With the silting up of the River Dee and the decline of Chester as a port in the early 19th century, Neston began to thrive as a market town and coaching station.

NESTON
The Old Mill c1940 N88002

This lovely old building stands in Leighton Road, close to its junction with Wood Lane. There are records of millers in Neston dating back to 1672, and the Mostyn Estate map of 1814 indicates two windmills in the area, but one was demolished in 1822 following severe storm damage. The sails of the mill last turned towards the end of the 1880s, but from 1975 to 1990 it had a new lease of life when it became home to a glass engraving business. It has since been renovated with a new roof and turned into a lovely one-bedroom residence by the owner, Mr Blackburn, who lives in the cottage just visible to the right of the mill.

PARKGATE, *The Front c1960* P255042

This view along The Parade at Parkgate has changed very little over the intervening years. All of the houses still stand. The Old Quay Inn, to the right, is still trading, and so are the majority of the shops along the front. One change, however, is the demise of the slender spire in the centre of the picture.

PARKGATE
The Red Lion Inn
c1960 P255031

The town of Parkgate has a
rather fascinating history. It
started as a small, coastal
hamlet occupied by a few
fishermen and shrimpers. It
then evolved into a bustling
sea port during the 18th
century, and finally, before
the tide ceased to lap
against the sea wall, it
developed into a
fashionable seaside resort.
Encroaching sands and
developing salt marsh put
paid to both the shipping
and sun-worshipping
trades, and today Parkgate
serves as a pleasant
commuter town. However,
it still retains the
atmosphere of a seaside
resort. The Red Lion Inn still
trades on The Parade.

PARKGATE
The Parade c1950
P255008

PARKGATE, *The Parade c1955* P255301

One of these very similar views shows the town on a bright summer day with the road thronged with vehicles and the pavements, benches and sea wall busy with visitors enjoying the Cheshire sunshine and the expansive views across the Dee Estuary. The second photograph depicts a virtually deserted Parkgate, but there is still evidence of a beach beneath the sea wall. The projecting section of promenade shown in both photographs is known as the Donkey Stand, because it was possible to take donkey rides along the sands from here as far as South Slip and back.

PARKGATE
The Boat House c1940
P255015

This building stands at the northern end of The Parade; it was built in 1926 on the site of a former coaching inn, the Pengwern Arms, which had to be demolished in 1885 following storm damage. It originally functioned as a café, serving visitors who chose to stroll along the promenade from the town or those who braved the cool seawater at Parkgate baths. The baths were situated just to the north of the Boat House, where Gayton Sands Nature Reserve car park now stands. The Boat House is now an inn and restaurant.

PARKGATE, *The Beach c1940* P255007

This is one of the final stretches of golden sand that once graced the foreshore at Parkgate before the estuary totally silted up and salt marsh encroached. Parkgate was a popular yachting centre. Some of the boys on the beach were probably from Mostyn House School in the town; the yacht in the foreground is a typical 12ft vessel favoured by the school.

► **PARKGATE**
Loading Mussels
1939 P255011

Wirral fishermen are loading mussels into jute sacks ready for transportation to the restaurants of Cheshire and Liverpool. The Boat House is visible at the end of The Parade. Though shellfish are still gathered by some locals from the brackish sands to the north of Parkgate, the commercial trade ceased when the estuary finally silted up in the 1950s.

◄ **HESWALL**
Pensby Road c1965
H276137

Pensby Road has changed little since the mid 1960s. The paving slabs on the right have been replaced with a swathe of tarmac, and the ornate clock (left) above Jones the chemist's has gone - the shop now sells floor coverings. However, The Rainbow news and sweet shop, on the left, is still trading.

▲ **HESWALL,** *Telegraph Road c1955* H276053

It is thought that the name Telegraph Road comes from a 19th-century telegraph station that stood on top of the Beacons, to the west of the road; but if that was the case, it was not part of the telegraph system used for shipping, as most such stations on the Wirral were.

◄ **HESWALL**
Telegraph Road c1965
H276156

This photograph is similar to H276053, and was taken from outside Castle Buildings. The old building on the right, which still houses Lloyds bank, dates from the early 1900s. In 1990 the local council had plans to demolish this fine structure in order to improve traffic flow through Heswall – we may be thankful that permission was refused. The trees on the grass verge are now much bigger, and tend to obscure the view along the road.

HESWALL
Dee View Road c1955
H276049

The No 14 bus chugs up Dee View Road from Heswall Village, passing the Dee View Inn on the right, which stands on the junctions of Dee View Road, The Mount and Dawstone Road. The photograph was taken at the war memorial on the edge of the park. The shop on the left is now a house, and the Co-op to its right no longer trades either.

HESWALL
The Children's Hospital c1965
H276144

The Royal Liverpool Children's Hospital, Heswall was opened in 1911 on a 9-acre site bordering Telegraph Road. The hospital originally had a series of open air wards (not visible here) to the rear of the building, with one side of each ward being totally open to the elements. The philosophy at the time was that fresh air would help clear congested lungs, particularly with diseases such as TB. The wards were later enclosed when opinions about the nation's health changed. The hospital closed in 1985 and was demolished in 1989; a Tesco supermarket now occupies the site.

HESWALL, *School Hill c1955* H276047

This view was taken from the top of School Hill, looking across the Dee Estuary towards the Clwydian Hills. Trees now obstruct the view of Heswall parish church, whose tower we can clearly see here. St Peter's School stands at the top of School Hill. During May 1941, Heswall was bombed, the school lost three classrooms and the headmaster's daughter and her fiancé were killed. The shop on the right is advertising Player's cigarettes - they probably killed a few people too!

HESWALL
The Village c1955
H276068

HESWALL, *The Village c1955* H276051

These two photographs, taken in Village Road, depict the old village centre. The scene has changed remarkably little over the years, apart from what is sold in the shops. The small, ornate castellated building in the centre of the row of shops used to be Heswall Village Post Office, but that later moved to its present position in the building to its immediate right. In the photograph it is occupied by Keegan's shoe shop, but it now houses an art and craft shop.

► **THURSTASTON**
Beach Path c1950
T174005

This path descends onto Thurstaston Sands alongside Shore Cottage. When Parkgate, further down the Dee, was inaccessible owing to the state of the tide, ships would tie up and unload at a small anchorage just off-shore from here known as Dawpool. During this time, the customs officers who would check the various cargoes being unloaded occupied the cottage.

► **THURSTASTON**
The Church c1955
T174007

The first mention of St Bartholomew's church dates back to 1125, and that structure survived until 1820. It was replaced by a fairly plain church, which was largely demolished in 1885. This rather splendid edifice took its place, constructed of warm, honey-coloured stone beneath a rich red tile roof. The Ismay family used the church - they founded the White Star Line Shipping Company, of which the *Titanic* was the most famous yet ill-fated vessel.

THURSTASTON, *A View of the Welsh Hills c1950* T174006

This splendid view from Thurstaston Hill looks over the village, with the spire of St Bartholomew's church projecting above the trees and roof tops. Thurstaston Hill is furnished with a trig point, a well placed bench and a brass map that points out places visible from this fine vantage point. Considering that it is just shy of 300 feet above sea level, the panorama is quite spectacular, with the Clwydian Hills, on the far side of the Dee Estuary, being particularly obvious. The plinth and map were erected in honour of Andrew Blair, founder of the Liverpool and District Federation of the Ramblers Association in 1923.

◄ **THURSTASTON**
The Cottage Loaf
c1955 T174002

This shows the Cottage Loaf as tea rooms, for which purpose it was built in 1930. The ethos of the owners was to supply the public with old-fashioned home baking and cooking in a comfortable and pleasant environment. The building still stands on the eastern side of the A540, close to Thurstaston, but it is now a very attractive and well cared-for inn, with manicured lawns, picnic benches and a mass of brightly coloured flower baskets and tubs.

THE NORTH WIRRAL SHORELINE

WEST KIRBY, *Grange Road c1965* W170017

'Kirkby', from which West Kirby derives its name, was established by a small group of Scandinavian settlers in the 10th century. The church, or kirk, that they founded here was dedicated to St Bridget, a famous Irish virgin. This photograph is taken close to the junction with Dee Lane. The fine building on the left was occupied by Martins Bank in the mid 1960s. It still functions as a bank, but under the Barclays banner.

31

WEST KIRBY
Banks Road c1965
W170060

This scene, looking north along Banks Road from the corner of Eaton Road, has changed very little in recent years. There is still a newsagents on the corner with Alexandra Road on the left. Fahy's, on the opposite corner, is now Hector's Sandwich Shop, and the paving slabs have been replaced with a rather attractive combination of red bricks in white flags.

33

◄ **WEST KIRBY**
The Promenade c1965
W170054

The boathouse on the left was built in 1903. When this photograph was taken, the Reliance Motor Engineering and Yachting Co Ltd occupied the left-hand half of the building. They specialised in marine engines, boat repairs, trolley making and welding. The whole of the building has now gone, to be replaced with a modern structure that dispenses all the familiar fast-food items of seaside resorts.

◀ **WEST KIRBY**
The Park c1965
W170051

Sandlea Park nestles in the centre of West Kirby, but the swings, see-saw and climbing frame have long gone, probably as a result of EU health and safety regulations. The park is now a well cared-for green oasis, with manicured lawns, footpaths fringed with lovely flower beds and shrub borders, and a number of benches.

▲ **WEST KIRBY,** *The Promenade c1965* W170045

We are looking south along West Kirby's busy Promenade, with the marine lake to the right. The lake was built at a cost of £2,500; it was due to open on 14 October 1899, but severe weather intervened, and the opening was cancelled for one week. It is still a very popular venue, with yachts and dinghies sailing across its enclosed waters and the brightly coloured sails of wind-surfers zipping across its surface. At the far end of the Promenade is the world famous West Kirby Sailing Club.

◀ **HOYLAKE**
Market Street c1960
H277056

We are looking west along Market Street from the corner of Cable Road, a scene that has changed remarkably little, apart from a big increase in the volume of traffic, especially on sunny weekends and holiday periods. The ornate canopy over the pavement on the left still shelters pedestrians from rain (and sun), but the shop is now a café called Ruby rather than a shoe shop. The clock on the wall of the building at the end of the row still tells the good people of Hoylake the time too.

► **HOYLAKE**
Market Street
c1965 H277055

This photograph was taken in the other direction to H277056 (page 35), looking east along Market Street. The name Hoylake refers to Hoyle Lake, a deep-water anchorage just off the shore and favoured by ships transporting cargoes of goods and passengers either along the Dee Estuary or into Liverpool. By the time the lake silted up in the 1830s, the name Hoylake had replaced Hoose, the original name of the village that nestled in the sand-hills on the fringes of Liverpool Bay. The attractive building on the left is St Luke's Methodist church.

◄ **HOYLAKE**
The Yachts c1960
H277008

This busy scene shows yachts being rigged ready to sail and others with their sails full as their occupants enjoy the fresh sea air of Liverpool Bay. Hoylake is still a very popular destination for yachtsmen and women, who now sail largely in fibreglass-hulled vessels rather than in the wooden ones seen here.

▲ **HOYLAKE,** *The Swimming Pool c1965* H277010

The original Hoylake baths were opened in June 1913, and were filled by the sea flowing over a low sea wall. However, this caused problems with the condition of the bathing water, with various bits of flotsam, jetsam, sand and mud washing into the baths. New baths (the ones we see here) were built in 1931, and they proved extremely popular; the English National Championships were held here. The baths were closed and demolished in 1984.

◀**GREAT MEOLS**
The Parade c1965
M191056

Little has changed here over the years, apart from more robust material being added to the sea defences along The Parade. The promenade footpath was built in the late 1800s so that the increasing number of visitors and holiday-makers could enjoy the 'curative powers of the sea air'.

GREAT MEOLS
*The Dinghy Slipway
c1965* M191061

This busy scene was taken near Dove Point slipway, and shows the increasing attraction of the area as a sailing centre. With the building of the railway in 1866, prosperous businessmen from Birkenhead and Liverpool moved to this part of the north Wirral coast. Hotels and guest-houses were built, and the number of holiday-makers seeking pleasure in Meols and Hoylake increased significantly.

39

GREAT MEOLS
Station Approach
c1950 M191015

GREAT MEOLS, *Station Approach c1955* M191027

This row of shops with their protective glass awnings was built in the grounds of Cleveley Lodge (the building at the far left end of the row) in the 1930s. The front of Cleveley Lodge was also extended at the time to accommodate the post office and a chemist's shop. The buildings stand beneath the Birkenhead Road where it spans the railway line near Meols Station. The canopies and shops are still there, but all have changed: a kitchen company, a Chinese restaurant and a mini-supermarket now trade from the site.

GREAT MEOLS
The Railway Inn c1965
M191052

This pub should technically be called The New Railway Inn, because it stands on the site of a former inn of the same name. The original inn could not be demolished until the new pub was built, because at the time the licence had to be transferred from one premises to the other without a break in trading. The 'new' Railway Inn opened along Birkenhead Road on 1 December 1938, allowing the old inn to be pulled down and the site turned into a car park.

GREAT MEOLS, *St John's Church c1965* M191047

The foundation stone of this very attractive red brick building was laid on 21 October 1911 by Lord Derby, and the church was finally consecrated on 12 April 1913. It stands on the junction of Forest Road and Birkenhead Road, and is most imposing, thanks to its turrets and ornate brick and tile work. The most highly perfumed roses enliven the olfactory senses as you approach the main doorway to the church.

▼ **MORETON,** *The Lighthouse c1965* M192023

The light last beamed out across Liverpool Bay on 15 July 1908, when the last keeper was a Mrs Williams, the only known woman lighthouse keeper of her time. After a period as a tearoom, the building remained derelict until 1989, when it was restored and converted into an information centre and Ranger Office for the North Wirral Coastal Park.

► **WALLASEY**
St Nicholas' Church c1960
W164025

This fine church in Wallasey Village is also known locally as the Harrison Memorial Church, because it was built as a memorial by the Harrison children for their parents, James and June Harrison. Messrs Harrison gave Harrison Park to the people of Wallasey as a gift in 1896. The church still stands in Bayswater Road at its junction with Groveland Road.

◀ WALLASEY
Liscard
Roundabout c1960
W164048

This is a part of
Wallasey known as
Liscard Village. The
roundabout was
removed in 1979 to
make way for a new
road junction. The
road directly ahead is
now pedestrianised
with attractive brick
and stone flag
walkways, benches,
trees and ornate
lanterns draped with
flower baskets.
Martin's Bank (left) is
now Barclays, and
some of the buildings
on the right have been
demolished and
replaced with more
modern ones.

▶ WALLASEY
The Village c1900
W164301

The photographer
was standing at the
top of Leasowe Road
at its junction with
Wallasey Village. The
mode of transport at
this time was horse-
drawn carriage or
Shank's pony; the
horses were well
catered for in Wallasey
Village, as we can see
from the drinking
trough encircling the
lamp post in the
middle of the road.

► **WALLASEY**
The Village c1955
W164006

Like W164301 (page 43), this was taken from Leasowe Road, but from the opposite corner some fifty-five years later. The ornate lamp-post and drinking trough have gone, to be replaced by bollards and a zebra crossing. The large black and white half-timbered building, with the bus stops outside, is the Black Horse Inn, which still stands. The building to its left has been demolished to create a car parking area, and the ornate clock on the wall of W Sumpter's stationer's shop (left) is also, unfortunately, a thing of the past.

◄ **WALLASEY**
The Village c1955
W164004

We are looking north along Wallasey Village, with the bollards at the top of Leasowe Road visible on the left. The cobbled street to the immediate left, just beyond the chemists, is Lycette Road. The cobbles have long since been covered over, but there is still a pharmacy trading from the same premises. The attractive spire on the building on the right has gone, although the main body of the building remains.

▲ **WALLASEY,** *The Village c1965* W164083

Some ten years later than W164006 and W164004 (page 44), this photograph looks south along Wallasey Village with Leasowe Road going off to the right. The bollards and zebra crossing have gone, to be replaced by a large floral roundabout, and the road has been considerably widened with the demolition of some buildings. Tesco (centre) is now an interior design shop.

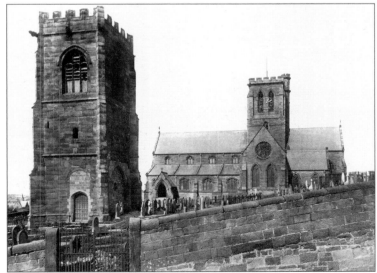

WALLASEY
The Church and the Tower c1895
36682

The history of St Hilary's church spans the centuries since the Norman Conquest, and it may even go back to the earliest days of Christianity in Britain. The first church here was built by Robert d'Avranches, one of William the Conqueror's barons. The tower in the foreground is all that remains of the fourth church, which was built in 1530. It was destroyed by fire in 1857: by the time someone had raced to Birkenhead to alert the fire brigade, and they had harnessed the horses to the fire tenders and galloped back to Wallasey, little remained of the church apart from a charred shell and the tower. The tower has recently been renovated, and is due to open to the public as part of a Heritage Trail.

WALLASEY
*St Hilary's Church
c1950* W164501

Following the devastating fire of 1857, a room was rented in the Ship Inn for Sunday worship until a new church could be built. Our predecessors, building in an age of great material prosperity, decided that a building adequate to meet the needs of the future could hardly be built around the old tower because it would dwarf it. The new church now stands on the highest point of Hilary's Brow, and was built from stone donated by Mrs Maddock from her quarry in Rake Lane. The church was dedicated on 28 July 1859, only two and a half years after the fire.

WALLASEY
Victoria Road c1910
W164311

This photograph, taken towards the eastern end of Victoria Road, shows what an important retail area this was. Most of the shops on the right have awnings pulled down to protect their wares and produce from the sun. The pavement outside many of the outlets also acts as an extension to the windows, with various items on display. Two of the ornate pavilions on New Brighton pier can just be seen at the far end of the road.

WALLASEY, *May Cottage and the Nook 1898* W164012

This late Victorian scene is typical of many of the towns and villages in England at the time. A horse-drawn cart delivering coal in jute sacks stands outside Edwards' the decorators, while the coal-man sits on the empty coal sacks and sucks on his pipe while the photograph is taken. Notice the old gas light outside May Cottage.

WALLASEY, *The Village 1895* W164008

This scene in Wallasey Village, near the junction with St John's Road, shows an old thatched cottage typical of the time. Notice that the window next to the door appears to be covered in, probably to avoid paying window tax. The cottage became a garage in later years, but it was demolished in the 1930s. The children in the foreground are pressed tight against the wall, maybe in apprehension, as photographs at this time were a rare event.

49

► **WALLASEY**
The Docks c1965 W164086

Wallasey Docks were built on what was known as Wallasey Pool, a once wild and beautiful tidal creek. The first boiler-making and shipbuilding yard was built by William Laird, the Liverpool-based Scotsman, in the mid 1820s. In 1829 he launched his first iron ship, a 60-ton lighter for use in Ireland. Dock development in Wallasey Pool continued at a pace from then on, with Egerton and Morpeth Docks opening in 1847, Alfred Dock being finished in 1851 and Wallasey Dock opening in 1877.

NEW BRIGHTON
The Royal Iris approaching the Pier c1960 N14021

The ferry *Leatown* can be seen tied up alongside the pier, while the *Royal Iris* waits to dock. The *Iris* and her sister ship, the *Daffodil*, entered ferry service in 1906. During the First World War they saw action as troop carriers in the raid on Zeebrugge, and after the war the prefix *Royal* was added in recognition of their wartime service. In later years, both vessels were sold and became cruise ships. The *Royal Iris* worked the Mersey and Liverpool Bay waters until the 1990s, when she went to Cardiff and was decommissioned.

NEW BRIGHTON, *The Swimming Pool c1960* N14031

There were two swimming pools in New Brighton. The Harrison Drive Baths were opened in 1932 by Lord Derby, and were hence known as the Derby Baths. The New Brighton Swimming Pool opened in 1934 and became very popular with visitors. At the time of its construction, it was thought to be the largest bathing pool in the world, accommodating 2,000 bathers and 10,000 spectators.

▼ **NEW BRIGHTON,** *The Pier Band c1870* N14307

This shows one of the pier pavilions with the pier band playing to visitors arriving at the pier head on one of the Mersey ferries. The photograph was taken shortly before the single-storey buildings on top of the sea wall were demolished to make way for 'Ham and Egg Parade'.

► **NEW BRIGHTON** *'Ham and Egg Parade' c1890* N14302

In the early 1870s, a Manchester syndicate built the long terraced row we see here. The single-storied Lower Parade had shops, restaurants and various refreshment stops, with a terraced walkway above giving access to the Higher Parade. The building soon became known as 'Ham and Egg Parade' because of a popular dish served in the restaurants.

◄ **NEW BRIGHTON**
The Pier 1900
45166

Not only did New Brighton attract vast numbers of visitors from Liverpool and Lancashire, but also hawkers too. They would arrive on an early ferry with their wicker baskets and 'set up shop' along the promenade or on the beach. They would try to peddle such things as rock, drinks, postcards, paper windmills, shells, beads and flowers. A group of such ladies can be seen here seated on the promenade (left).

► **NEW BRIGHTON**
The Pier 1900 45165

New Brighton was originally conceived as 'The sea-bathing rendezvous par excellence of the Lancashire people of note', but things soon went awry. By 1857 it had virtually become a suburb of Liverpool, with the resort being invaded by the working classes and not by its intended patrons, the members of the industrial aristocracy and bourgeoisie.

NEW BRIGHTON
The Pier c1890 N14303

Promenade Pier was opened in 1867; it was built beside the Ferry Pier, which connected New Brighton directly with Liverpool. 70 feet wide and 550 feet long, the pier was a classic of its type, featuring a pavilion where numerous sideshows and events could be seen. However, the pier was dependant on visitors, and once the ferry service from Liverpool ceased in 1971 its days were numbered. The turnstiles ceased turning, and the pier closed; it was finally demolished in 1978.

NEW BRIGHTON, *The Pier c1875* N14304

The original pier was designed by Eugenius Birch, and was one of the classic piers of the British seaside resort in its design. There is a three-phase regeneration plan for New Brighton seafront, which includes the building of a new 500 ft long pier on the site of the previous one.

NEW BRIGHTON, *The Tower 1898* 40902

The New Brighton Tower was completed in 1898, about eight years after the Blackpool Tower. Standing at 560 feet, it was 42 feet higher than Blackpool Tower, and the tallest structure in England at the time. It afforded magnificent views of the Isle of Man, the Welsh mountains and the Lakeland fells from the viewing platform at the top.

▶ NEW BRIGHTON
The Tower 1900 45173

The tower was part of a 35-acre development that also included Tower Buildings and Tower Gardens. The whole complex was a focal point of entertainment, with a theatre, ballrooms, a roller-rink, snooker rooms, a skating rink, a menagerie, various refreshment stalls, an aviary, a monkey house and a lake with gondolas.

▼ NEW BRIGHTON
The Beach c1960 N14025

This photograph shows Tower Buildings (right) minus the tower, which was dismantled between 1919 and 1921. The Tower Buildings continued to attract the crowds until 1969, when the remaining structure, included the famous Tower Ballroom, was destroyed by fire.

NEW BRIGHTON
Victoria Gardens and New Promenade c1915 48655a

NEW BRIGHTON, *Victoria Gardens, the Pier and the Promenade c1915* 48659a

The Victoria Gardens, seen here soon after they were opened by Lord Derby in 1913, were built on the site of the infamous 'Ham and Egg Parade', which had gained a scandalous reputation for rowdiness, vulgarity, insobriety and prostitution. By ridding itself of this embarrassing eyesore and replacing it with this green oasis, New Brighton was hoping to attract the sort of visitor that it had initially envisaged would come to the resort.

NEW BRIGHTON
The Lighthouse 1892
30413

The foundation stone of the New Brighton lighthouse was laid on 8 June 1827 by Thomas Littledale, Mayor of Liverpool. It became known as Perch Rock Lighthouse because the reef of rock on which it stands (seen here at low tide) once had a post or 'perch' placed on it to warn shipping of its location.

▶ **NEW BRIGHTON**
The Lighthouse
1895 36680

This photograph shows the lighthouse at high tide with the reef virtually submerged. The light was powered by sperm whale oil. It shone for the last time in 1973, when it was sold to a local businessman who installed mains electricity and converted the building into a holiday retreat. It was sold again in 1974.

◀ **EGREMONT**
The Promenade 1912
64440

A family walk down Magazine Lane Slipway onto the beach. This is close to the site of the magazines: ships entering the Mersey had to deposit any gunpowder there during their stay in port. In 1851 the magazines were transferred to vessels anchored in the Mersey. Little sand remains on this section of shoreline today, and the cobbles of the slipway are covered in concrete.

▲ **EGREMONT,** *Vale Park 1912* 64437

Vale Park was created in 1898 from the grounds of two previous estates, Liscard Vale Hall and The Woodlands. The Hall was the home of the Holland family, who filled the grounds with many of the fine trees, shrubs and plants that were collected during their extensive world travels. Although the tower can no longer be seen, Vale Park is still a pleasant green space used by locals and visitors alike.

◄ **EGREMONT**
From the Sands 1895
36686

Apart from the clothes that these three youngsters are wearing on the beach, little has changed here. There are more stones on the beach now, and the house in the background, Mere Bank, which is now part of an exclusive housing development, is obscured by mature trees.

EGREMONT, *The Promenade 1912* 64432

We are looking along Egremont's Promenade towards New Brighton from Tobin Street. The spire to the left of New Brighton Tower belonged to the Liverpool Home for Aged Mariners, but like the tower, it too has gone. Large stone groynes now jut out into the Mersey from the Promenade in an attempt to stop wave erosion.

EGREMONT
The Promenade 1912 64433

This is a similar photograph to 64432 (page 64), but taken from Egremont Ferry. This was the second section of promenade to be constructed, with work beginning in 1891. Before this, the river frontage would have been largely open to the shore.

EGREMONT, *The Promenade 1912* 64439

This photograph looks south along the Promenade to Egremont Ferry. A large iron pier and landing stage once projected out into the Mersey to the left of the picture. The ferry buildings on the left have now gone, and the area is now a small car park with excellent views across the river to Liverpool.

THE MERSEY SHORELINE

BIRKENHEAD
Hamilton Square 1967 B399039

The ornate building with the crowning clock tower is Birkenhead Town Hall, designed by C O Ellison & Son of Liverpool. Its foundation stone was laid in 1883, and the building opened in 1887. The original clock tower was destroyed by fire in 1901, and replaced by the one we see here. The building now houses the Wirral Museum.

BIRKENHEAD
Charing Cross 1967
B399044

We are looking along Grange Road from the corner of Oxton Road. The ornate building on the right, occupied by the Midland Bank at the time this photograph was taken, is still there, but it is now Hamiltons, a pub and wine bar. Grange Road is now fully pedestrianised, a MacDonald's stands on the site of the Grange Hotel (left), and the roundabout has gone.

► **BIRKENHEAD**
The Clock Tower
c1965 B399025

The King Edward VII
Memorial Clock
stands outside the
Central Hotel in
Clifton Crescent. It
originally stood on
the corner of Argyle
Street and Grange
Road, but it was
moved to its present
location in 1929 in
order to make way for
the Mersey Tunnel
approach roads.

◄ **BIRKENHEAD**
The Library 1962
B399035

The Library was opened
on 18 July 1934 by King
George V and Queen
Mary, who also opened
the Queensway Mersey
Tunnel on the same day.
This white limestone
building has changed
little over the years, but
Borough Road, in which
it stands, is now a busy
dual carriageway.

▲ **BIRKENHEAD,** *Woodchurch Road c1955* B399004

This photograph was taken on the outskirts of Birkenhead in Prenton. The road leading off to the left is Moss Road, which is now blocked off to form a cul-de-sac, and the bollards and ornate lantern (centre) have gone. The Birkenhead and District Co-operative Society shop on the corner now holds a conservatory showroom.

◄ **BIRKENHEAD**
The Ferry and the Bus Terminus 1964 B399032

This busy scene was taken at the Woodside ferry and bus terminus. The original 'ferry across the Mersey' was operated by monks from Birkenhead Priory, a little way to the south of the present terminus. The buildings that are shown here have all been replaced in recent years - and so have the buses!

◄ BROMBOROUGH
The Cross c1965
B445033

Bromborough is an ancient settlement that dates back to Saxon times when King Alfred's daughter, Ethelfleda, had a monastery built here. The base of the cross probably dates back to the late 1200s, and would have acted as the focal point for most village activities. A new shaft with an ornate capital was added in 1874.

◄ **BROMBOROUGH**
Raby Mere c1955
B445007

Raby Mere lies two miles east of the village of Raby, and has always been a popular Wirral destination, especially with Sunday School outings. By damming the River Dibbins, this man-made mill pool was created to provide water for the corn mill that once stood nearby.

▲ **PORT SUNLIGHT,** *Lever House c1960* P188077

For generations, Lever House has accommodated the main offices of Lever Brothers. Lever ensured that although they were closely linked, the factory and the village did not intrude on one another. It is difficult to believe that a vast factory complex lies behind this rather elegant stone façade. The royal coat of arms above the main entrance is a reminder of the 'By Appointment' royal patronage awarded to the company by Queen Victoria.

PORT SUNLIGHT
The Post Office c1960
P188071

The post office is the black and white half-timbered building on the left. Immediately to the left, but out of shot, is the Gladstone Theatre, which was opened as Port Sunlight's first public building by W E Gladstone in 1891. The building on the extreme right was the village library when this photograph was taken, but it is now the Heritage Centre and Information Office.

PORT SUNLIGHT
Dell Bridge c1955
P188038

This is one of many fine examples of public amenity open space in Port Sunlight. Dell Bridge was built in 1894 to span what was once the upper reaches of Dell Creek, a former tidal creek that once divided the village in half. It was drained and landscaped and now forms a lovely green ribbon through Port Sunlight.

PORT SUNLIGHT, *The Bowling Greens c1960* P188087

Lever employed thirty different architects to create Port Sunlight's unique style. Not only was he an avid believer in property sharing, but he also believed that the well-being of the community went hand-in-hand with its success. To try and maximise this belief he introduced many schemes for the welfare, education and entertainment of his workers. The bowling greens here in Bolton Road are just one example.

PORT SUNLIGHT
Hulme Hall c1965
P188088

Construction of Hulme Hall began on 5 March 1900, and it was opened on 29 July 1901. It was built to serve as the women's dining hall, and could seat almost two thousand people. During the evening it doubled as the village hall. During the First World War it served as a military hospital for wounded soldiers.

PORT SUNLIGHT, *The Bridge Inn c1965* P188091

The Bridge Inn is named after Victoria Bridge, built to span a tidal creek that ran across the line of Bolton Road; the bridge thus linked Bolton Road to the New Chester Road (the creek was eventually filled in and the bridge buried). The Bridge Inn was opened as a hotel in 1900, but traded initially on wholly temperance lines, which meant no alcohol. This state of affairs continued until a referendum was held amongst the villagers in 1903: they voted 4:1 in favour of a drinks licence for the building. Sensible people!

PORT SUNLIGHT
The Memorial c1965
P188093

PORT SUNLIGHT, *The Memorial and the Art Gallery c1960* P188105

The war memorial, unveiled in 1921, was designed by Sir William Boscombe John, and stands on the site of Port Sunlight's old gymnasium. It is a unique and dramatic representation of the sufferings of the whole of society. The centrepiece, a large granite cross, is surrounded by eleven bronze figures symbolising the defence of the home. The circular parapet surrounding the cross has two bronze panels on either side of the four flights of steps, which depict children presenting floral garlands in token of gratitude. There are four more bronze panels set between these representing sea, land and air forces and the Red Cross. Inscribed in stone round the rim of the parapet is: 'Their names shall remain and forever their glory shall not be blotted out'.

PORT SUNLIGHT
The Lady Lever Art Gallery c1960 P188085

The gallery contains Lord Leverhulme's world-famous collection of pre-Raphaelite paintings and Wedgwood pottery. By allowing the residents of Port Sunlight and the thousands of visitors who come here a chance to share this art collection, Leverhulme not only created a wonderful memorial to his late wife but also ensured a lasting gift to the nation.

PORT SUNLIGHT, *The Gardens and the Fountains c1955* P188014

The fountain and pond are situated at the front of the art gallery at the end of a ribbon of lawns and rose beds known as the Diamond. 'Sea Piece' is the name of the bronze from which water sprays; it depicts a legendary sea-horse with a triton and baby triton astride its back. It was sculpted by Sir Charles Wheeler, and it was switched on in July 1950.

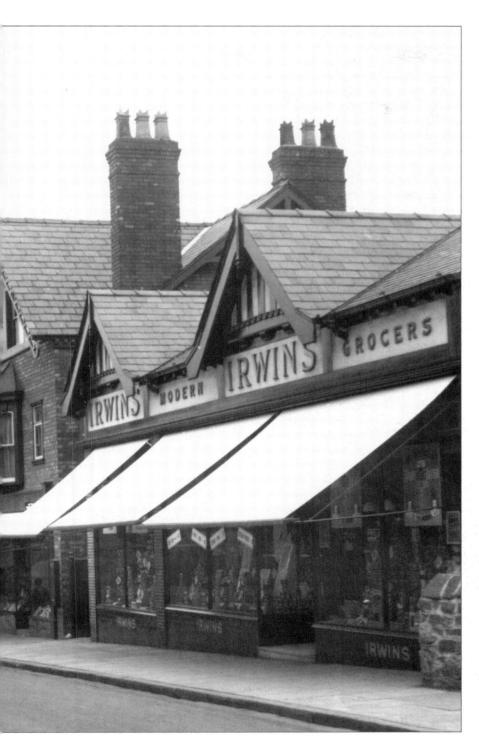

BEBINGTON
The Village c1955 B660014

Taken across the road from the
Wellington Inn, this view is
looking south along the village.
Bebington cum Bromborough
became a civil parish in 1922
when Bromborough, Higher
Bebington and Lower Bebington
were united. Irwin's Grocery
shop is now occupied by a
barber's, a ladies' hair salon and
an electronics shop. The shops
to the left have been converted
into private dwellings.

BEBINGTON, *St Andrew's Church c1955* B660027

St Andrew's church, in Church Lane, has served this ancient parish for hundreds of years. Registers of baptisms from 1558 to 1961, of marriages from 1558 to 1971 and of burials from 1558 to 1909 from the church are at the County Records Office, along with many transcripts of monumental inscriptions.

80

BEBINGTON
*Wirral Grammar
School for Boys c1955*
B660014a

Situated in Heath Road,
Wirral Grammar School for
Boys was officially opened
on 26 September 1931, at
the same time as an almost
identical building, Wirral
Grammar School for Girls,
was opened round the
corner in Cross Lane. The
main building has changed
little externally, but new
extensions have been
added to cope with
expanding populations and
new educational trends.

BEBINGTON, *Teehey Lane c1955* B660033

The town owes much to the Victorian jeweller Joseph Mayer, who gave his home village a little library in Mayer Hall in 1866.
The grounds behind the hall became a public park, with a small museum exhibiting fine art and crafts, mainly from Ancient
Egypt. The spire at the far end of Teehey Lane is that of Christ Church.

▶ **BEBINGTON**
Broadway c1955
B660034

We are looking east along Broadway towards the road junction with King's Road and King's Lane. The floral roundabout still controls traffic flow, and the shops on the left still trade, but now as a dry cleaner's and a travel agent's.

◀ **BEBINGTON**
Brackenwood Gardens c1950
B660022

Brackenwood House, shown here covered in Virginia creeper, dates back to the 1880s. It was purchased by Bebington Council in the 1920s for use as council offices. In the 1970s, a large 18-hole golf course was built to replace a small 9-hole course, and part of the house became a golf club.

▲ **BEBINGTON,** *Mayer Park c1950* B660018

This photograph looks across Mayer Park from the terrace of Mayer House. The park still serves as a peaceful oasis for the people of Bebington. The ornate pots have gone from the top of the steps, and many of the flower beds have been replaced with shrubs. The trees are also much taller today, creating a mature-looking landscape.

◄**EASTHAM**
The Ferry 1887 20062

This view northwards along the Mersey shoreline towards Eastham Pier shows one of the Mersey ferries alongside. The iron pier was built in 1874 by the lessees of the Eastham Ferry Hotel, obviously with an eye to improving their own trade as well as that of the village.

EASTHAM
The Village c1955
E90007

The photographer was standing outside St Mary's parish church and looking towards The Hooton Arms, the white-painted building at the end of the road (right). The inn was built in 1852, originally as the schoolmaster's house adjoining the new village school, but by 1860 it had become a public house.

▼ **EASTHAM,** *Chester New Road c1955* E9035

The village of Eastham is about one mile inland from the River Mersey, but one of its claims to fame is that it has the largest canal locks in the country - these give entry to the Manchester Ship Canal.

▶ **EASTHAM**
Queen Elizabeth Docks c1955 E9018

The tanker *Languedoc* is tied up at Eastham's Queen Elizabeth Docks. The docks were constructed in the 1950s next to the entrance of the Manchester Ship Canal, replacing a series of old docks and wharfs. Many of the ships that dock here are oil tankers for the adjacent oil refinery.

◄ EASTHAM
Queen Elizabeth Docks c1955 E9020

To the left, and above the bow of the tanker *Dauphine*, we can see the huge lock gates that give access to the Manchester Ship Canal. The canal was opened on 1 January 1894. It became known as 'The Big Ditch' during its construction, but when completed it allowed ocean-going vessels to sail the 35 miles to Salford Docks, close to the heart of Manchester.

► EASTHAM
The Docks 1894 33716

A ship is sailing along the Manchester Ship Canal towards the old docks in Eastham in the same year that the canal was opened. Work began on the canal in 1887, and at its peak 97 steam excavators, 174 locomotives, 6,300 trucks, 194 cranes, 212 steam pumps, 59 pile engines, 196 horses and 16,000 navvies were involved. However, only 15,870 of the navvies were able to clock off at the end of their final shift; 130 lost their lives, and countless others lost fingers, hands, toes, feet and whole limbs in the harsh and dangerous conditions that prevailed.

ELLESMERE PORT
Christ Church c1955
E135008

Christ Church is seen
here from Station Road,
at the time when the vicar
was the Reverend E M B
Southwell. The church
was built in 1869 at a cost
of £2,900 and replaced an
earlier church.

ELLESMERE PORT, *The Refineries from Canal Bridge c1955* E135011

Ellesmere Port was the focal point for much of the canal activity in Cheshire. The Shropshire Union Canal, shown here, links
the heavily industrialised Midlands with the River Mersey at Ellesmere Port. Some of the old mills and warehouses
alongside the canal have been given a new lease of life with the development of the Boat Museum.

ELLESMERE PORT
The Corporation Offices c1955 E135015

Whitby Hall, seen here, was built in Stanney Lane by the Grace family in the 1860s. In 1931 it was purchased by the council, who used the building as offices. It still stands, with the surrounding grounds transformed into a park; the house is now used by numerous clubs and societies. The ivy has been stripped off, and a café is now situated round the back.

ELLESMERE PORT, *Whitby Road c1955* E135018

We are looking east along Whitby Road, with Vale Road meeting it on the opposite side. The wall and trees on the left have now gone, and the Sportsman's pub now stands here. The row of shops is still there, but Mellor's baker's shop (centre) is now a locksmiths; the shops with awnings outside are now a florist's and the offices of the TGWU.

ELLESMERE PORT
Station Road c1955
E135041

This view looks along
Station Road at its junction
with Westminster Road (on
the left) and Meadow Lane.
The Westminster Bank
building (left) still stands,
but it is now occupied by a
bookmaker's. The buildings
on the right of Station Road,
which include the
Hippodrome, Barclays Bank
and the Public Library, have
all been demolished.

TOWNS AND VILLAGES OF THE INTERIOR

WILLASTON, *The Green c1950* W371024

The Green has always been a focus for village life, and has several fine old buildings surrounding it. The posts have now gone, but there is still a bench; and the copper beech tree, just visible on the left, is now a fine, mature specimen that shades much of the Green. The building with the two cars parked outside is The Nag's Head (formerly The White Lion), which dates from the first part of the 1700s.

WILLASTON
The Old Hall and the Smithy c1940 W371003

The Hall is situated close to the village green along Hadlow Road. This imposing three-storey building is constructed from red brick, and has an Elizabethan-style front that includes three tall gables that we can clearly see here. It is thought that it dates from the 17th century, despite a date-stone carved over the door which is inscribed 'HB 1558'. The small village smithy on the right has now gone.

WILLASTON, *The Green Lantern c1950* W371002

This building in Neston Road, with its ornate green lantern above the main entrance, once served as a café. It has recently been renovated, along with many of the farm buildings to the rear, and now forms part of the Delamere Farm complex; this is a development of twelve exclusive and high specification homes.

WILLASTON
The Village c1965
W371042

We are looking along Neston Road from outside Christ Church, with the entrance to the Green Lantern café on the left. Aston's shop (right) still trades under the same name, but it is now Aston's Tea Rooms.

▼ **WILLASTON,** *The Mill c1950* W371006

This is Wirral's tallest mill at 80 feet; it is constructed from materials salvaged from mills that had previously stood on the site. The first records of a mill here go back to 1321, but it is not known exactly how many mills have stood here in the intervening years to 1800, when the present mill was built. Following storm damage in 1930 when the sails were destroyed, the mill became obsolete. It now forms part of a private residence.

► **LITTLE SUTTON**
Chester Road c1965
L558044

Little Sutton lies just north-west of Ellesmere Port, and in recent years, along with Great Sutton, it has more or less coalesced with it. The village straddles the main A41 Chester Road with the main shopping area spread out in a linear fashion on either side of the road, as we can see here.

◄ LITTLE SUTTON
Ledsham Road c1965 L558050

This photograph shows Ledsham Road close to its junction with Chester Road. The scene has changed remarkably little over the years, apart from the names above the shops. The small lean-to building on the left has gone, and a Chinese restaurant occupies the site; the road junction is now furnished with traffic lights.

► LITTLE SUTTON
Rivacre Baths c1950
L558014

Rivacre Valley Swimming Pool was one of the main attractions within the 45-acre site that comprised Rivacre Valley. The diving area, at the far end of the pool, was totally separate from the main body of the baths, which were surrounded by well tended gardens, paved areas, benches and ornamental fountains. It was known as 'the swimming pool in a garden'. It closed about 20 years ago, and the baths were filled in. Only the old exit turnstile still remains.

▼ **HOOTON,** *The Memorial and the Church c1960* H363004

St Paul's church is a very fine building indeed, constructed in an Italianate style with contrasting bands of red and white sandstone and finished with an unusual octagonal spire. It was built between 1858 and 1862 for Mr R C Naylor, owner of Hooton Hall (now demolished) as a tribute to his wife. The columns and gate house to the right of the war memorial formed the main entrance to Hooton Hall, the grounds of which are now a golf course.

► **BURTON**
The Village c1960
B561032

The house with the two dormer windows in the roof on the left used to be The Stanley Arms, one of two hostelries that once refreshed the village. Its name comes from the Stanley Massey family who owned nearby Ness Colliery. It is now Stanley House.

◄ **BURTON**
The Village c1955
B561020

As with picture No B561032 (below), this is looking east along the village. Very little has changed, except that the unsightly telegraph poles have now gone, along with the shutters on St Nicholas House to the right. The photograph was taken from Rake Corner, where there is a delightful thatched cottage.

► **BURTON**
Manor College
c1960 B561052

Built in 1806 and known as Burton Hall, this gracious old building was considerably altered in the 1900s by the new owners of the Burton Estate, the Gladstone family, who also changed its name to Burton Manor. It is now a residential college for adult education.

BURTON
The Church c1960
B561027

The parish church of St Nicholas, like many of Wirral's fine buildings, is constructed from local red sandstone. The church dates mainly from 1721, but some features remind us that there were three or possibly more churches here before this one. The first stone church was erected soon after 1086 to cater for the spiritual needs of the families of the thirteen persons recorded in the Domesday Book.

BURTON, *View of Moel Fammau c1960* B561039

Burton is considered by many to be one of the most picturesque villages in the Wirral, and it is enhanced by the wonderful panorama over the Dee Estuary to the hills of Wales. The peak in the centre of the photograph is Moel Fammau, the highest mountain in the Clwydian Range at 1,821 feet.

RABY
The Wheatsheaf Inn c1950
R413001

This lovely thatched, half-timbered inn has stood on this site, alongside the connecting road from Birkenhead to Neston, since 1611. It must have been a welcome hostelry for many a weary traveller crossing the Wirral over the centuries, and it still provides a warm and friendly welcome to visitors today. The interior of the inn has changed somewhat over the years, but the general structure remains the same. The barn to the right has now been incorporated into the main part of the building and windows added.

THORNTON HOUGH, *The Village Smithy c1950* T221002

The present smithy was built in 1905 to replace the original one, which was demolished along with several other buildings in order to create space for the erection of St George's Congregational church, which stands a little further along Neston Road on the right. The smithy still stands, and looks much now as it did here, when it was occupied by T S Williams, 'Shoeing and General Smith'.

THORNTON HOUGH
Raby Road c1950
T221003

THORNTON HOUGH, *The Village c1950* T221004

This village is referred to as 'Torintone' in the Domesday book, but during the reign of Edward II it, and much of the surrounding land, came into the possession of Roger de Thornton, whose only daughter married Richard de Houghe, and hence it became 'Thornton Houghe'. The recent development of the village has been largely due to two men. The first was Joseph Hirst, a wealthy Yorkshire woollen manufacturer, who retired here in the 1860s and built his ideal home, Thornton House. He also built a village school, the parish church, the vicarage and the row of terraced cottages in Church Street. The second was William Hesketh, later Viscount Leverhulme, who came here from Bolton in 1887 and set up his soap factory at Port Sunlight. Not to be outdone by old Joseph Hirst, he too built a church and another school, and added the post office, the village club and a range of fine houses throughout the village. Today, Thornton Hough is a most attractive village that has been designated a Conservation Area, and has been awarded numerous 'Best kept village' awards.

GAYTON
The Devon Doorway c1955
G352011

This attractive building stands on Gayton Roundabout, at the junction of Barnston, Chester and Telegraph Roads. It was constructed as a small coaching cafe in 1930 by Mrs Aldridge, a lady from Devon, hence the name. It is now a thriving pub, surrounded by flower-filled borders, tubs and hanging baskets

BARNSTON, *Tree Cottage c1955* B441001

Barnston appears in the Domesday Book as 'Bernestone', then held by William Fitz-Nigel, second Baron of Halton. It is wrongly thought by some people that the settlement derived its name from a large granite boulder in the village known as the Barn Stone.

BARNSTON
The Fox and Hounds
c1955 B441003

The original inn that stood on this site dated from the 16th century, but it was dismantled in 1910 and the present inn built. It still looks the same as in this photograph, apart from a fresh white coat of paint and a new pub sign hanging from the wrought iron wall bracket.

IRBY, *Thigwall Road c1955* I42014

We are looking across Irby Road and along Thigwall Road. The lovely stone building on the extreme left is Manor Farm, which F C Beazley described in his book on Thurstaston as 'a little gem'; unfortunately, it has been demolished, and a rather incongruous-looking building that houses the Public Library now stands there.

IRBY
The Village c1955
I42005

IRBY, *The Village c1955* I42009

These two views look along Thigwall Road. The white-painted single-storey building in the middle of the row of shops originally had a thatched roof and was Irby's only shop, doubling also as the village post office. When the gable-ended building to its right was built, it became the Irby Stores run by Mr A Constantine, who was still trading when these photographs were taken. It is now a Bargain Store, and the old post office has been demolished, to be replaced by a new row of shops with flats above.

IRBY
The Village c1955
I42007

We are looking along Mill Hill Road from the Shippons, a large public house in Thigwall Road. Martins Bank is now occupied by a hair and beauty salon; although the Esso sign has gone, the Irby Motor Company still trades from the same premises. Mill Hill Road is still one way, but new 'no entry' signs mark its designation.

IRBY
Thurstaston Road c1955 142015

The Anchor Inn (left) is a solid sandstone building, and its contents have refreshed the inhabitants of Irby for over 100 years. In the 19th century and the early 1900s, it was one of two pubs that served the village. The other, The Prince of Wales, closed in the 1920s; it only had a licence to sell beer, unlike The Anchor, which had a full licence. There used to be a ship's anchor hanging from the wrought iron bracket (just visible beneath the public footpath sign), but that has gone, along with the single-storey building to the right.

IRBY
The Hall c1950 142004

Irby Hall was built on the site of the ancient manor house of St Werburgh's Abbey, Chester. The building dated from the early 17th century and was completely half-timbered. The present Irby Hall was reconstructed in 1888, with the half-timbering on the ground floor being replaced with sandstone, as we see here. The building looks much the same today, except for a row of old-fashioned street lamps lining the left-hand edge of the drive.

▲ **CALDY,** *The Church c1955* C356001

The lovely red sandstone Caldy parish church was opened on 1 November 1907 and dedicated to the Resurrection and All Saints. It replaced the former village chapel, which had been formed by converting outbuildings at Caldy Manor into a place of worship.

◄**CALDY**
The Village c1955
C356004

This view looks along Caldy Road with the part stone, part half-timbered Reading Room on the right. It was built by the Barton family in 1883. The estate of Caldy Manor was purchased by Mr R W Barton in 1832 for the then princely sum of £18,900. He was one of a number of wealthy Manchester merchants who settled in the Wirral.

CALDY, *The Village Cross c1955* C356002

Pevsner in *The Buildings of England* says of Caldy: 'Cheshire is something of a Surrey of the North, but Surrey has nothing to compare with this'. In 1906, the Caldy Manor Estate was split up into housing development plots for the wealthy. The smallest ones were about an acre in size, and this influenced the sorts of houses constructed during the Edwardian period; consequently the village reflects this glimpse of Edwardian elegance in its buildings.

UPTON
Ford Road c1960
U36014

We are looking west towards the cross-roads in the part of Upton known as The Village. Up until the end of the Second World War, Upton was a stand-alone village, but with urban expansion on the Wirral, it has coalesced with Woodchurch, Greasby and Moreton, so that now it is not a separate community any longer.

UPTON, *Ford Road c1960* U36015

Taken from the corner of Arrowe Park Road, this photograph is looking east along The Village. Traffic lights now stand on this corner, which is much busier today than in the relatively quiet days of motoring. The large stone building on the left is still there, but it is now a hair and beauty salon, not a tea shop.

▶ **UPTON**
*The Village and
the Church c1955*
U36008

Upton is an ancient settlement mentioned in the Domesday survey as 'Optone in Wilaveston Hundred'. (A hundred was an administrative unit within a county, and was named after its central meeting place, in this case Willaston). St Mary's parish church, on the left of Ford Road, is largely obscured by trees now, but the church clock still rings out the time to the people of Upton.

◀ **UPTON**
The Village c1960
U36018

Apart from the extra, more modern vehicles in Upton now, little has changed from this photograph. E J Clarke (right) is now a Balti House, the clock on the wall advertising sweets and ices has disappeared, and the shop beneath is now Central Pets. The black and white half-timbered building (centre) is the Eagle and Crown public house.

▲ **UPTON,** *St Joseph's Church c1960* U36021

St Joseph's Catholic church stands in Arrowe Park Road, just a short step from the main cross-roads in the village. It was designed by Adrian Scott and opened in 1954. Next year the church celebrates its half centenary. St Joseph's Catholic Primary School stands immediately to the right of the church.

◀ **UPTON**
Thermopylae Pass
c1950 U36001

This is a view from Bidston Hill, which was declared a place to be kept free of development when Birkenhead and the surrounding towns and villages began to grow. Until 1851 the hill was a mass of flagpoles, as signals were sent by semaphore all the way from Holyhead to Bidston. From here signals were sent by raising various flags into the port at Liverpool, so that ship owners could be made aware of their vessels' arrival.

BIDSTON, *The Windmill c1955* B443002

The windmill, which still stands on the summit of Bidston Hill, was built as a flour mill in 1800 and functioned as such until 1875. The tenuous fingers of decay and various storms caused much damage in the ensuing years, but it was restored and new sails were added in the 1990s. There are now frequent open days when the interior and the operating machinery can be seen.

INDEX

Frith Book Co Titles

www.francisfrith.co.uk

The Frith Book Company publishes over 100 new titles each year. A selection of those currently available is listed below. For latest catalogue please contact Frith Book Co.

Town Books 96 pages, approximately 100 photos. **County and Themed Books** 128 pages, approximately 150 photos (unless specified). All titles hardback with laminated case and jacket, except those indicated pb (paperback)

Amersham, Chesham & Rickmansworth (pb)	1-85937-340-2	£9.99	Devon (pb)	1-85937-297-x	£9.99
Andover (pb)	1-85937-292-9	£9.99	Devon Churches (pb)	1-85937-250-3	£9.99
Aylesbury (pb)	1-85937-227-9	£9.99	Dorchester (pb)	1-85937-307-0	£9.99
Barnstaple (pb)	1-85937-300-3	£9.99	Dorset (pb)	1-85937-269-4	£9.99
Basildon Living Memories (pb)	1-85937-515-4	£9.99	Dorset Coast (pb)	1-85937-299-6	£9.99
Bath (pb)	1-85937-419-0	£9.99	Dorset Living Memories (pb)	1-85937-584-7	£9.99
Bedford (pb)	1-85937-205-8	£9.99	Down the Severn (pb)	1-85937-560-x	£9.99
Bedfordshire Living Memories	1-85937-513-8	£14.99	Down The Thames (pb)	1-85937-278-3	£9.99
Belfast (pb)	1-85937-303-8	£9.99	Down the Trent	1-85937-311-9	£14.99
Berkshire (pb)	1-85937-191-4	£9.99	East Anglia (pb)	1-85937-265-1	£9.99
Berkshire Churches	1-85937-170-1	£17.99	East Grinstead (pb)	1-85937-138-8	£9.99
Berkshire Living Memories	1-85937-332-1	£14.99	East London	1-85937-080-2	£14.99
Black Country	1-85937-497-2	£12.99	East Sussex (pb)	1-85937-606-1	£9.99
Blackpool (pb)	1-85937-393-3	£9.99	Eastbourne (pb)	1-85937-399-2	£9.99
Bognor Regis (pb)	1-85937-431-x	£9.99	Edinburgh (pb)	1-85937-193-0	£8.99
Bournemouth (pb)	1-85937-545-6	£9.99	England In The 1880s	1-85937-331-3	£17.99
Bradford (pb)	1-85937-204-x	£9.99	Essex - Second Selection	1-85937-456-5	£14.99
Bridgend (pb)	1-85937-386-0	£7.99	Essex (pb)	1-85937-270-8	£9.99
Bridgwater (pb)	1-85937-305-4	£9.99	Essex Coast	1-85937-342-9	£14.99
Bridport (pb)	1-85937-327-5	£9.99	Essex Living Memories	1-85937-490-5	£14.99
Brighton (pb)	1-85937-192-2	£8.99	Exeter	1-85937-539-1	£9.99
Bristol (pb)	1-85937-264-3	£9.99	Exmoor (pb)	1-85937-608-8	£9.99
British Life A Century Ago (pb)	1-85937-213-9	£9.99	Falmouth (pb)	1-85937-594-4	£9.99
Buckinghamshire (pb)	1-85937-200-7	£9.99	Folkestone (pb)	1-85937-124-8	£9.99
Camberley (pb)	1-85937-222-8	£9.99	Frome (pb)	1-85937-317-8	£9.99
Cambridge (pb)	1-85937-422-0	£9.99	Glamorgan	1-85937-488-3	£14.99
Cambridgeshire (pb)	1-85937-420-4	£9.99	Glasgow (pb)	1-85937-190-6	£9.99
Cambridgeshire Villages	1-85937-523-5	£14.99	Glastonbury (pb)	1-85937-338-0	£7.99
Canals And Waterways (pb)	1-85937-291-0	£9.99	Gloucester (pb)	1-85937-232-5	£9.99
Canterbury Cathedral (pb)	1-85937-179-5	£9.99	Gloucestershire (pb)	1-85937-561-8	£9.99
Cardiff (pb)	1-85937-093-4	£9.99	Great Yarmouth (pb)	1-85937-426-3	£9.99
Carmarthenshire (pb)	1-85937-604-5	£9.99	Greater Manchester (pb)	1-85937-266-x	£9.99
Chelmsford (pb)	1-85937-310-0	£9.99	Guildford (pb)	1-85937-410-7	£9.99
Cheltenham (pb)	1-85937-095-0	£9.99	Hampshire (pb)	1-85937-279-1	£9.99
Cheshire (pb)	1-85937-271-6	£9.99	Harrogate (pb)	1-85937-423-9	£9.99
Chester (pb)	1-85937-382 8	£9.99	Hastings and Bexhill (pb)	1-85937-131-0	£9.99
Chesterfield (pb)	1-85937-378-x	£9.99	Heart of Lancashire (pb)	1-85937-197-3	£9.99
Chichester (pb)	1-85937-228-7	£9.99	Helston (pb)	1-85937-214-7	£9.99
Churches of East Cornwall (pb)	1-85937-249-x	£9.99	Hereford (pb)	1-85937-175-2	£9.99
Churches of Hampshire (pb)	1-85937-207-4	£9.99	Herefordshire (pb)	1-85937-567-7	£9.99
Cinque Ports & Two Ancient Towns	1-85937-492-1	£14.99	Herefordshire Living Memories	1-85937-514-6	£14.99
Colchester (pb)	1-85937-188-4	£8.99	Hertfordshire (pb)	1-85937-247-3	£9.99
Cornwall (pb)	1-85937-229-5	£9.99	Horsham (pb)	1-85937-432-8	£9.99
Cornwall Living Memories	1-85937-248-1	£14.99	Humberside (pb)	1-85937-605-3	£9.99
Cotswolds (pb)	1-85937-230-9	£9.99	Hythe, Romney Marsh, Ashford (pb)	1-85937-256-2	£9.99
Cotswolds Living Memories	1-85937-255-4	£14.99	Ipswich (pb)	1-85937-424-7	£9.99
County Durham (pb)	1-85937-398-4	£9.99	Isle of Man (pb)	1-85937-268-6	£9.99
Croydon Living Memories (pb)	1-85937-162-0	£9.99	Isle of Wight (pb)	1-85937-429-8	£9.99
Cumbria (pb)	1-85937-621-5	£9.99	Isle of Wight Living Memories	1-85937-304-6	£14.99
Derby (pb)	1-85937-367-4	£9.99	Kent (pb)	1-85937-189-2	£9.99
Derbyshire (pb)	1-85937-196-5	£9.99	Kent Living Memories(pb)	1-85937-401-8	£9.99
Derbyshire Living Memories	1-85937-330-5	£14.99	Kings Lynn (pb)	1-85937-334-8	£9.99

Available from your local bookshop or from the publisher

Frith Book Co Titles (continued)

Lake District (pb)	1-85937-275-9	£9.99	Sherborne (pb)	1-85937-301-1	£9.99
Lancashire Living Memories	1-85937-335-6	£14.99	Shrewsbury (pb)	1-85937-325-9	£9.99
Lancaster, Morecambe, Heysham (pb)	1-85937-233-3	£9.99	Shropshire (pb)	1-85937-326-7	£9.99
Leeds (pb)	1-85937-202-3	£9.99	Shropshire Living Memories	1-85937-643-6	£14.99
Leicester (pb)	1-85937-381-x	£9.99	Somerset	1-85937-153-1	£14.99
Leicestershire & Rutland Living Memories	1-85937-500-5	£12.99	South Devon Coast	1-85937-107-8	£14.99
Leicestershire (pb)	1-85937-185-x	£9.99	South Devon Living Memories (pb)	1-85937-609-6	£9.99
Lighthouses	1-85937-257-0	£9.99	South East London (pb)	1-85937-263-5	£9.99
Lincoln (pb)	1-85937-380-1	£9.99	South Somerset	1-85937-318-6	£14.99
Lincolnshire (pb)	1-85937-433-6	£9.99	South Wales	1-85937-519-7	£14.99
Liverpool and Merseyside (pb)	1-85937-234-1	£9.99	Southampton (pb)	1-85937-427-1	£9.99
London (pb)	1-85937-183-3	£9.99	Southend (pb)	1-85937-313-5	£9.99
London Living Memories	1-85937-454-9	£14.99	Southport (pb)	1-85937-425-5	£9.99
Ludlow (pb)	1-85937-176-0	£9.99	St Albans (pb)	1-85937-341-0	£9.99
Luton (pb)	1-85937-235-x	£9.99	St Ives (pb)	1-85937-415-8	£9.99
Maidenhead (pb)	1-85937-339-9	£9.99	Stafford Living Memories (pb)	1-85937-503-0	£9.99
Maidstone (pb)	1-85937-391-7	£9.99	Staffordshire (pb)	1-85937-308-9	£9.99
Manchester (pb)	1-85937-198-1	£9.99	Stourbridge (pb)	1-85937-530-8	£9.99
Marlborough (pb)	1-85937-336-4	£9.99	Stratford upon Avon (pb)	1-85937-388-7	£9.99
Middlesex	1-85937-158-2	£14.99	Suffolk (pb)	1-85937-221-x	£9.99
Monmouthshire	1-85937-532-4	£14.99	Suffolk Coast (pb)	1-85937-610-x	£9.99
New Forest (pb)	1-85937-390-9	£9.99	Surrey (pb)	1-85937-240-6	£9.99
Newark (pb)	1-85937-366-6	£9.99	Surrey Living Memories	1-85937-328-3	£14.99
Newport, Wales (pb)	1-85937-258-9	£9.99	Sussex (pb)	1-85937-184-1	£9.99
Newquay (pb)	1-85937-421-2	£9.99	Sutton (pb)	1-85937-337-2	£9.99
Norfolk (pb)	1-85937-195-7	£9.99	Swansea (pb)	1-85937-167-1	£9.99
Norfolk Broads	1-85937-486-7	£14.99	Taunton (pb)	1-85937-314-3	£9.99
Norfolk Living Memories (pb)	1-85937-402-6	£9.99	Tees Valley & Cleveland (pb)	1-85937-623-1	£9.99
North Buckinghamshire	1-85937-626-6	£14.99	Teignmouth (pb)	1-85937-370-4	£7.99
North Devon Living Memories	1-85937-261-9	£14.99	Thanet (pb)	1-85937-116-7	£9.99
North Hertfordshire	1-85937-547-2	£14.99	Tiverton (pb)	1-85937-178-7	£9.99
North London (pb)	1-85937-403-4	£9.99	Torbay (pb)	1-85937-597-9	£9.99
North Somerset	1-85937-302-x	£14.99	Truro (pb)	1-85937-598-7	£9.99
North Wales (pb)	1-85937-298-8	£9.99	Victorian & Edwardian Dorset	1-85937-254-6	£14.99
North Yorkshire (pb)	1-85937-236-8	£9.99	Victorian & Edwardian Kent (pb)	1-85937-624-X	£9.99
Northamptonshire Living Memories	1-85937-529-4	£14.99	Victorian & Edwardian Maritime Album (pb)	1-85937-622-3	£9.99
Northamptonshire	1-85937-150-7	£14.99	Victorian and Edwardian Sussex (pb)	1-85937-625-8	£9.99
Northumberland Tyne & Wear (pb)	1-85937-281-3	£9.99	Villages of Devon (pb)	1-85937-293-7	£9.99
Northumberland	1-85937-522-7	£14.99	Villages of Kent (pb)	1-85937-294-5	£9.99
Norwich (pb)	1-85937-194-9	£8.99	Villages of Sussex (pb)	1-85937-295-3	£9.99
Nottingham (pb)	1-85937-324-0	£9.99	Warrington (pb)	1-85937-507-3	£9.99
Nottinghamshire (pb)	1-85937-187-6	£9.99	Warwick (pb)	1-85937-518-9	£9.99
Oxford (pb)	1-85937-411-5	£9.99	Warwickshire (pb)	1-85937-203-1	£9.99
Oxfordshire (pb)	1-85937-430-1	£9.99	Welsh Castles (pb)	1-85937-322-4	£9.99
Oxfordshire Living Memories	1-85937-525-1	£14.99	West Midlands (pb)	1-85937-289-9	£9.99
Paignton (pb)	1-85937-374-7	£7.99	West Sussex (pb)	1-85937-607-x	£9.99
Peak District (pb)	1-85937-280-5	£9.99	West Yorkshire (pb)	1-85937-201-5	£9.99
Pembrokeshire	1-85937-262-7	£14.99	Weston Super Mare (pb)	1-85937-306-2	£9.99
Penzance (pb)	1-85937-595-2	£9.99	Weymouth (pb)	1-85937-209-0	£9.99
Peterborough (pb)	1-85937-219-8	£9.99	Wiltshire (pb)	1-85937-277-5	£9.99
Picturesque Harbours	1-85937-208-2	£14.99	Wiltshire Churches (pb)	1-85937-171-x	£9.99
Piers	1-85937-237-6	£17.99	Wiltshire Living Memories (pb)	1-85937-396-8	£9.99
Plymouth (pb)	1-85937-389-5	£9.99	Winchester (pb)	1-85937-428-x	£9.99
Poole & Sandbanks (pb)	1-85937-251-1	£9.99	Windsor (pb)	1-85937-333-x	£9.99
Preston (pb)	1-85937-212-0	£9.99	Wokingham & Bracknell (pb)	1-85937-329-1	£9.99
Reading (pb)	1-85937-238-4	£9.99	Woodbridge (pb)	1-85937-498-0	£9.99
Redhill to Reigate (pb)	1-85937-596-0	£9.99	Worcester (pb)	1-85937-165-5	£9.99
Ringwood (pb)	1-85937-384-4	£7.99	Worcestershire Living Memories	1-85937-489-1	£14.99
Romford (pb)	1-85937-319-4	£9.99	Worcestershire	1-85937-152-3	£14.99
Royal Tunbridge Wells (pb)	1-85937-504-9	£9.99	York (pb)	1-85937-199-x	£9.99
Salisbury (pb)	1-85937-239-2	£9.99	Yorkshire (pb)	1-85937-186-8	£9.99
Scarborough (pb)	1-85937-379-8	£9.99	Yorkshire Coastal Memories	1-85937-506-5	£14.99
Sevenoaks and Tonbridge (pb)	1-85937-392-5	£9.99	Yorkshire Dales	1-85937-502-2	£14.99
Sheffield & South Yorks (pb)	1-85937-267-8	£9.99	Yorkshire Living Memories (pb)	1-85937-397-6	£9.99

See Frith books on the internet at www.francisfrith.co.uk

FRITH PRODUCTS & SERVICES

Francis Frith would doubtless be pleased to know that the pioneering publishing venture he started in 1860 still continues today. Over a hundred and forty years later, The Francis Frith Collection continues in the same innovative tradition and is now one of the foremost publishers of vintage photographs in the world. Some of the current activities include:

Interior Decoration

Today Frith's photographs can be seen framed and as giant wall murals in thousands of pubs, restaurants, hotels, banks, retail stores and other public buildings throughout the country. In every case they enhance the unique local atmosphere of the places they depict and provide reminders of gentler days in an increasingly busy and frenetic world.

Product Promotions

Frith products are used by many major companies to promote the sales of their own products or to reinforce their own history and heritage. Frith promotions have been used by Hovis bread, Courage beers, Scots Porage Oats, Colman's mustard, Cadbury's foods, Mellow Birds coffee, Dunhill pipe tobacco, Guinness, and Bulmer's Cider.

Genealogy and Family History

As the interest in family history and roots grows world-wide, more and more people are turning to Frith's photographs of Great Britain for images of the towns, villages and streets where their ancestors lived; and, of course, photographs of the churches and chapels where their ancestors were christened, married and buried are an essential part of every genealogy tree and family album.

Frith Products

All Frith photographs are available Framed or just as Mounted Prints and Posters (size 23 x 16 inches). These may be ordered from the address below. From time to time other products - Address Books, Calendars, Table Mats, etc - are available.

The Internet

Already fifty thousand Frith photographs can be viewed and purchased on the internet through the Frith websites and a myriad of partner sites.

For more detailed information on Frith companies and products, look at these sites:

www.francisfrith.co.uk
www.francisfrith.com
(for North American visitors)

See the complete list of Frith Books at:

www.francisfrith.co.uk

This web site is regularly updated with the latest list of publications from the Frith Book Company. If you wish to buy books relating to another part of the country that your local bookshop does not stock, you may purchase on-line.

For further information, trade, or author enquiries please contact us at the address below:
The Francis Frith Collection, Frith's Barn, Teffont, Salisbury, Wiltshire, England SP3 5QP.
Tel: +44 (0)1722 716 376 Fax: +44 (0)1722 716 881   Email: sales@francisfrith.co.uk

See Frith books on the internet at www.francisfrith.co.uk

FREE MOUNTED PRINT

Mounted Print
Overall size 14 x 11 inches

Fill in and cut out this voucher and return
it with your remittance for £2.25 (to cover postage and handling). Offer valid for delivery to UK addresses only.

Choose any photograph included in this book.
Your SEPIA print will be A4 in size. It will be mounted in a cream mount with a burgundy rule line (overall size 14 x 11 inches).

**Order additional Mounted Prints
at HALF PRICE (only £7.49 each*)**
If you would like to order more Frith prints from this book, possibly as gifts for friends and family, you can buy them at half price (with no additional postage and handling costs).

Have your Mounted Prints framed
For an extra £14.95 per print* you can have your mounted print(s) framed in an elegant polished wood and gilt moulding, overall size 16 x 13 inches (no additional postage and handling required).

---

* IMPORTANT!

These special prices are only available if you order at the same time as you order your free mounted print. You must use the ORIGINAL VOUCHER on this page (no copies permitted). We can only despatch to one address.

Send completed Voucher form to:
The Francis Frith Collection, Frith's Barn, Teffont, Salisbury, Wiltshire SP3 5QP

CHOOSE ANY IMAGE FROM THIS BOOK

Voucher for **FREE** and Reduced Price Frith Prints

Please do not photocopy this voucher. Only the original is valid, so please fill it in, cut it out and return it to us with your order.

Picture ref no	Page no	Qty	Mounted @ £7.49	Framed + £14.95	Total Cost
		1	Free of charge*	£	£
			£7.49	£	£
			£7.49	£	£
			£7.49	£	£
			£7.49	£	£
			£7.49	£	£

Please allow 28 days for delivery

* Post & handling (UK)	£2.25
Total Order Cost	£

Title of this book . . . .

I enclose a cheque/postal order for £ . . . .
made payable to 'The Francis Frith Collection'

OR please debit my Mastercard / Visa / Switch / Amex card
(credit cards please on all overseas orders), details below

Card Number

Issue No (Switch only)   Valid from (Amex/Switch)

Expires   Signature

Name Mr/Mrs/Ms . . . .
Address . . . .
. . . .
. . . .
. . . . Postcode . . . .
Daytime Tel No . . . .
Email . . . .

Valid to 31/12/05

Free Print – see overleaf

Would you like to find out more about Francis Frith?

We have recently recruited some entertaining speakers who are happy to visit local groups, clubs and societies to give an illustrated talk documenting Frith's travels and photographs. If you are a member of such a group and are interested in hosting a presentation, we would love to hear from you.

Our speakers bring with them a small selection of our local town and county books, together with sample prints. They are happy to take orders. A small proportion of the order value is donated to the group who have hosted the presentation. The talks are therefore an excellent way of fundraising for small groups and societies.

Can you help us with information about any of the Frith photographs in this book?

We are gradually compiling an historical record for each of the photographs in the Frith archive. It is always fascinating to find out the names of the people shown in the pictures, as well as insights into the shops, buildings and other features depicted.

If you recognize anyone in the photographs in this book, or if you have information not already included in the author's caption, do let us know. We would love to hear from you, and will try to publish it in future books or articles.

Our production team

Frith books are produced by a small dedicated team at offices in the converted Grade II listed 18th-century barn at Teffont near Salisbury, illustrated above. Most have worked with the Frith Collection for many years. All have in common one quality: they have a passion for the Frith Collection. The team is constantly expanding, but currently includes:

Jason Buck, John Buck, Douglas Mitchell-Burns, Ruth Butler, Heather Crisp, Isobel Hall, Julian Hight, Peter Horne, James Kinnear, Karen Kinnear, Tina Leary, David Marsh, Sue Molloy, Kate Rotondetto, Dean Scource, Eliza Sackett, Terence Sackett, Sandra Sampson, Adrian Sanders, Sandra Sanger, Julia Skinner, Lewis Taylor, Shelley Tolcher and Lorraine Tuck.